30 Million Different Insects in the Rain Forest

PAUL ROCKETT

Perspectives is published by Raintree, Chicago, Illinois, www.capstonepub.com

Library of Congress Cataloging-in-Publication Data
Rockett, Paul, author.
30 million different insects in the rain forest / Paul Rockett.
    pages cm.—(The big countdown)
Summary: "Can you count the animal species found in the rain forest or the fish in the Amazon River? Find out all about the rain forest, including its extraordinary variety of plant and animal life, its peoples, its layered structure, and its role as an oxygen producer, as well as why it's so important to protect."—Provided by publisher.
  Includes bibliographical references and index.
  ISBN 978-1-4109-6876-0 (library binding)
  ISBN 978-1-4109-6883-8 (paperback)
  ISBN 978-1-4109-6897-5 (ebook PDF)
1. Rain forests—Juvenile literature.
2. Rain forest conservation—Juvenile literature.
3. Rain forest animals—Juvenile literature.
4. Habitat conservation—Juvenile literature.
I. Title. II. Title: Thirty million different insects in the rain forest.

QH541.5.R27R63 2016
577.34—dc23   2014025332

Author: Paul Rockett
Illustrator: Mark Ruffle

Originally published in 2014 by Franklin Watts.
Copyright © Franklin Watts 2014.
Franklin Watts is a division of Hachette Children's Books, a Hachette UK company.
www.hachette.co.uk

Every attempt has been made to clear copyright. Should there be any inadvertant omission please apply to the publisher for rectification.

Picture credits: Adstock/Shutterstock: 17tl; Ryan M Bolton/Shutterstock: front cover c. Dirk Ercken/Shutterstock: 26tcr; Rui Ferreira/Shutterstock: 25c; guentermanaus/Shutterstock: 15cl; Rob Hainer/Shutterstock: 26tcl; Hamster Man/Shutterstock: 15cr; Hartl/blickwinkel/Alamy: 7br; Piter Hason/Shutterstock: 17tlb; Steffen Hauser/botanikfoto/Alamy: 17; Ron Haviv/VII/Corbis: 10bl; Anton Ivanov/Shutterstock: 18bl; JBK/Shutterstock: 28br; Kjersti Joergensen/Shutterstock: 19ccl; Wolfgang Kaehler/Corbis: 8tl; Andrew Karivny/Shutterstock: 19cl; Cynthia Kidwell/Shutterstock: 18br; Anna Kucherova/Shutterstock: 18bcr; Lightpoet/Shutterstock: front cover tr; Liquid Productions/LLC/Shutterstock: 15c; Alfredo Maiquez/Shutterstock: 26tr; Nagel Photography/Shutterstock: 19cr; Nella/Shutterstock: 4cl; Leon P/Shutterstock: 18bcl; Al Pidgin/Shutterstock: 20cl; Poetic Penguin/Shutterstock: 19ccr; Alexander Potapov/Shutterstock: 28bc; Mike Price/Shutterstock: 20tl; Dr Morley Read/Shutterstock: 4tl, 12bl, 14t, 26tl; David Reilly/Shutterstock: 17cl, 17clb, 17bl; reptiles4all/Shutterstock: 26cl; worldswildlifewonders/Shutterstock: 29tl, 29c; Pan Xunbin/Shutterstock: 17cla; S Zefei/Shutterstock: front cover bcl.

Throughout the book you are given data relating to various pieces of information covering the topic. The numbers will most likely be an estimation based on research made over a period of time and in a particular area. Some other research may reach a different set of data, and all these figures may change with time as new research and information is gathered. The numbers provided within this book are believed to be correct at the time of printing.

Printed in China.

CONTENTS

COUNTING DOWN THE RAIN FOREST   4

30 MILLION DIFFERENT INSECTS IN THE RAIN FOREST   6

3.4 MILLION MILES² (8.9 MILLION KM²) OF TROPICAL RAIN FOREST   8

700 THOUSAND TRIBAL PEOPLE IN BRAZIL   10

73,715 U.S. SOCCER FIELDS DESTROYED EACH DAY   12

HOW LONG IS THE AMAZON RIVER?   14

3,000 EDIBLE FRUITS   16

260 DIFFERENT SPECIES OF MONKEY   18

137 PLANT, ANIMAL, AND INSECT SPECIES DIE EACH DAY   20

88% HUMIDITY   22

28% OF THE WORLD'S OXYGEN   24

15-YEAR LIFE SPAN OF THE POISON DART FROG   26

FOUR LAYERS OF THE RAIN FOREST   28

FURTHER INFORMATION AND LARGE NUMBERS   30

GLOSSARY   31

INDEX   32

COUNTING DOWN THE RAIN FOREST

What is a rain forest?

Rain forests are so-called because they are dense patches of forest that receive a large amount of rain.

THERE ARE TWO TYPES OF RAIN FOREST:

○ **TROPICAL**

Tropical rain forests are found around the equator and are constantly warm and humid.

● **TEMPERATE**

Temperate rain forests are found outside the tropics near coastlines and experience colder weather than tropical rain forests.

Tropic of Cancer

Equator

Tropic of Capricorn

COUNTING THE RAIN FORESTS

Within rain forests there are areas of land that have yet to be explored and a large amount of wildlife that has yet to be discovered.

Scientists will estimate the number of creatures and plants within the rain forest. They do this because the amount of wildlife is too great to count individually and because a lot of rain forest life is still unknown.

An estimate is a prediction based upon experience and information available at the time. Estimates are used to demonstrate the size and variety of rain forest life, often to give an idea of what they contain within a scale that we might understand.

IT IS ESTIMATED THAT A 0.4 MILE² (1 KM²) AREA OF THE RAIN FOREST CONTAINS AS MANY AS:

144 species of flowering plant
72 species of tree
39 species of bird
14 species of butterfly
12 species of mammal
10 species of reptile
8 species of amphibian.

These estimates are based on smaller areas of rain forest where the content is able to be counted.

0.4 MILE²

0.4 MILE²

WHAT IS A SPECIES?

Species refers to a type of being. If there are eight species of amphibian in **0.4 mile²** (1 km²), there aren't just eight amphibians, but eight different types of amphibians, of which there may be a varying number.

0.4 mile² is an area that covers the same amount of space that is **0.4 mile²** in both width and length.

The Amazon rain forest area is **2,123,561 miles²** (5.5 million km²).

There are more insects in the rain forest than anywhere else in the world. New species are being discovered all of the time. There are around **1,000,000** insects that have been officially recorded, but many scientists estimate that there are actually **30,000,000** different insect species just in the rain forests.

THERE ARE SEVEN INSECT GROUPS. THEY ARE:

DRAGONFLIES

GRASSHOPPERS AND LOCUSTS

ANTS

TRUE BUGS

BUTTERFLIES AND MOTHS

BEES AND WASPS

BEETLES

NUMBER OF SPECIES IN INSECT GROUPS

2,000
4,000
6,000
8,000
10,000
12,000
14,000
≈
50,000
100,000
150,000
200,000
250,000
300,000
350,000
400,000

TRUE BUGS?

All insects are often called bugs, but true bugs are a group of bugs that is different from other insects. The main difference is that they suck! They have a long, tube-like beak through which they suck in food.

RAIN FOREST STUDY

In a study of rain forest insects, **100 different species** of ant have been found living in one tree. **700 different species** of beetle have also been found in **one tree**.

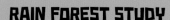

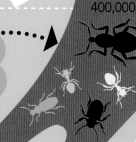

10,000,000,000,000,000,000 (10 quintillion) individual insects alive at any one time.

There are **400,000,000** different species of beetle; **20,000** of these are longhorn beetles. The largest beetle in the world is the titan beetle, which is from the longhorn beetle family.

THE TITAN BEETLE
THE WORLD'S BIGGEST
BEETLE

Titan beetles live deep in some of the world's hottest tropical jungles. Adults can grow to as long as **6.5 inches** (16.7 cm). Their jaws are strong enough to snap a pencil in half and damage a person's skin.

NUMBER OF SPECIES

400,000
300,000
200,000
100,000

20,000
15,000
10,000
5,000
0

BEETLE **LONGHORN BEETLE**

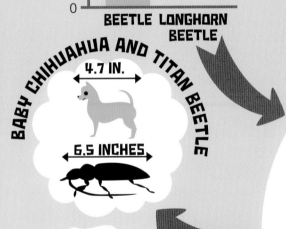

BABY CHIHUAHUA AND TITAN BEETLE

4.7 IN.

6.5 INCHES

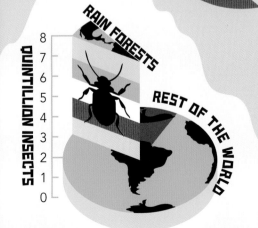

QUINTILLION INSECTS

8
7
6
5
4
3
2
1
0

RAIN FORESTS

REST OF THE WORLD

TITAN BEETLE

80% live in the rain forests. That means **8,000,000,000,000,000,000** (8 quintillion) individual insects live in **6%** of the world.

3.4 MILLION MILES² (8.9 MILLION KM²) OF TROPICAL RAIN FOREST

Millions of years ago the majority of the land on Earth was rain forest. 50,000,000 years ago Antarctica was warm enough to be considered as an area of rain forest and is believed to have been covered with plant life. Today, Antarctica is the coldest place on Earth—so cold that no trees are able to grow there.

RAIN FORESTS ON EARTH 50,000,000 YEARS AGO

▶ ANTARCTICA

Archaeologists have uncovered fossils of wood and ferns from Antarctica that are not too different from those found in rain forests today.

The world has changed a lot over **50,000,000 years**. Areas of land have shifted, breaking up to become the countries and continents we now have. The world's climate has also changed with the creation of different climate zones.

RAIN FORESTS ON EARTH TODAY

Tropical rain forests have a tropical climate with an average temperature of **64.4°F** (18°C).

Antarctica is described as having a polar climate. The average temperature here is **−70.6°F** (−57°C).

Earth's surface: **57,506,055 miles²** (148,940,000 km²)

Today, rain forests cover **3,450,363 miles²** (8,936,400 km²) of Earth's surface.

THE EARTH

Water: **70.8%**
Land: **29.2%**
Tropical rain forests: **6%**

6%

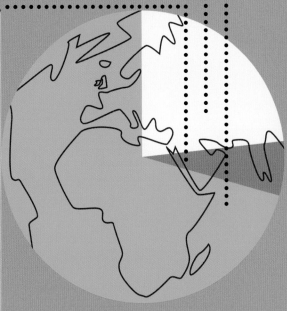

● Temperate rain forests cover
113,268 miles² (293,362 km²) of Earth.

○ Tropical rain forests cover
3,337,096 miles² (8,643,038 km²) of Earth.

THREE CLIMATE ZONES

Earth's climates are affected by the movement and shape of Earth. The curve of Earth and the tilt on its axis as it rotates mean that some parts of Earth receive more Sun than others. The temperatures of the wind and ocean currents also add to the conditions within each climate zone.

○ **TEMPERATE** climates have cold winters and mild summers with year-round rain.

○ **TROPICAL** climate zones are hot all year and some are also very wet.

○ **POLAR** climate zones are extremely cold and dry with long, dark nights.

700 THOUSAND
TRIBAL PEOPLE IN BRAZIL

Tribal people rely on natural resources for survival and can live in extreme environments that can be treacherous for those who have not grown up there. It's believed that there are still some tribes that remain undiscovered, and so the exact number of tribes and tribal people around the world is unknown.

IN THE RAIN FORESTS OF BRAZIL THERE ARE ESTIMATED TO BE:

700,000
tribal people in
200
different tribes
speaking a total of
170
languages.

AMAZON RAIN FOREST

The Yanomami tribe
Population: **32,000**

The Yanomami are the largest tribe living in the Amazon rain forest. They have special reserves of land set aside for them so that they can continue their traditional existence. The land covers **23,722,120 acres** in Brazil (twice the size of Switzerland) and **20,509,750 acres** in Venezuela.

POPULATION OF SWITZERLAND:
7,909,000

YANOMAMI POPULATION:
32,000

10

THE AKUNTSU TRIBE

Population: **5**

The Akuntsu are the smallest known tribe living in the Amazon rain forest. During the 1980s and '90s, the Akuntsu tribe suffered violent attacks by land developers, and now only five members remain. They live in a small patch of forest surrounded by huge cattle ranches and plantations—places that used to be home to their once-large tribe.

TRIBAL THREATS In Brazil alone, **90 tribes** are known to have been wiped out.

The tribes live in harmony with the rain forest.

The tribes' land is destroyed by developers. Some attack the tribes and bring with them new germs and diseases.

With their habitat taken from them and diseases and developers killing them, the tribes become extinct.

YANOMAMI TRIBE TIMELINE

50,000,000 years ago
The Yanomami tribe are believed to have been living in the Amazon rain forest for over **50,000,000 years**.

1940s
The Yanomami tribe were first discovered in the 1940s. Their encounter with people from the outside world led to many deaths from measles and flu.

1970s
In the 1970s bulldozers drove through their territory, building roads enabling the deforestation of their land.

1980s
In the 1980s **40,000 gold miners** invaded their land. Many villages were destroyed and native people shot. **20%** of the Yanomami died in just **seven years** during this period.

1990s
In 1992 Brazil recognized the Yanomami tribe's right to land, marking an area as the Yanomami Park. However, a year later, outsiders invaded and killed many of the tribe.

2000s–2014
Over **1,000 gold miners** are reported to be working illegally on Yanomami land. They are spreading diseases like malaria and polluting the rivers and forests with mercury. The tribe's health is suffering and medical care is not immediately available to them.

HOW THEY LIVE

The Yanomami tribe live in large circular houses, some of which can house up to **400 people**. Men hunt for food while women tend gardens and grow crops.

The Yanomami have a huge knowledge of plants within the rain forest and use about **500 plants** for food, medicine, house-building, and tools.

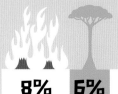

73,715 U.S. SOCCER FIELDS DESTROYED EACH DAY

Today, tropical rain forests cover 6% of Earth's land; 50 years ago they covered 14%.

8%	6%	

100% LAND SURFACE

If this rate of disappearance were to continue, in another **50 years** there would be no rain forest left.

The removal of trees from the rain forest is called deforestation.

CAUSES OF DEFORESTATION:

Subsistence farming: **48%**
Commercial agriculture: **32%**
Logging: **14%**
Fuel wood removal: **5%**

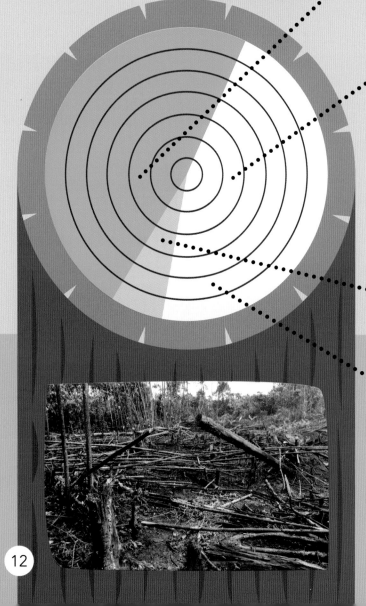

SUBSISTENCE FARMING is when farmers and tribes grow enough food to feed their immediate community. It involves a slash-and-burn technique of cutting down trees and burning forests. The land is only farmed for a short period of time before moving on to another area of land.

COMMERCIAL AGRICULTURE is when big companies develop land on a large scale to grow crops and graze cattle to sell. Single crops tend to be grown, which removes the diversity of nutrients in the soil. Fertilizers are also used, which pollute the soil. Land is also cleared to keep and rear livestock such as chickens and pigs. These animals are eventually sold. In the Brazilian rain forests, land has been cleared for:

700 million chickens	220 million cows	60 million pigs	20 million goats

LOGGING is when trees are cut down and used for furniture and construction. Within the rain forest, large areas are destroyed to create access roads to logging sites, and large trees are dragged over the forest floor.

FUEL WOOD REMOVAL is when trees are cut down for use as fuel. This is done on a large scale by mining and construction companies.

EFFECTS

The effects of all of these actions leave the rain forest soil dry and infertile. This makes it unlikely that any trees will be able to grow again on that land to replace the trees that were destroyed.

TO SCALE

To highlight the scale of destruction caused to the rain forests, many reports refer to the size not in miles^2 but with familiar objects and places. This may give us a better chance of understanding the actual scale.

AN AREA THE SIZE OF ENGLAND IS DESTROYED EACH YEAR.

A popular unit of measurement used when talking about rain forests is U.S. soccer fields. The use of this unit is more for suggestive scale than accuracy.

WITHIN THE TROPICAL RAIN FORESTS:

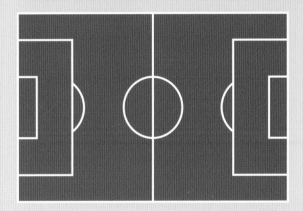

26,905,975 soccer fields are destroyed each year.

73,715 soccer fields are destroyed each day.

4.26 soccer fields are destroyed every five seconds.

Earth is around **4,600,000,000 years old**. If we were to scale that to **46 years**, humans have been here for just **four hours**, and the Industrial Revolution began just **one minute** ago.

In that time we've destroyed **50%** of the world's forests.

HOW LONG IS THE AMAZON RIVER?

The Amazon River is the second longest river in the world.

The Nile River is **4,132 miles** (6,650 km) long. The Amazon River is **4,000 miles** (6,400 km) long.

THE AMAZON RIVER HAS MORE TRIBUTARIES THAN ANY OTHER RIVER IN THE WORLD.

A TRIBUTARY is a stream that flows into a river. The Amazon River has more than **200 tributaries**.

TROPICAL RAIN FORESTS have some of the largest rivers in the world:

AMAZON RIVER:
4,000 miles (6,400 km)

MEKONG RIVER, CHINA:
2,703 miles (4,350 km)

ORINOCO RIVER, SOUTH AMERICA:
1,330 miles (2,140 km)

CONGO RIVER, AFRICA: 2,920 miles (4,700 km)

THE AMAZON RIVER carries more water than any other river in the world. It is responsible for **25%** of the fresh water that flows into the oceans.

THE AMAZON BASIN
The Amazon basin is covered by the Amazon rain forest. All of the water that collects within this area is drained into the Amazon River through its tributaries. It drains an area of about **2,669,896 miles²** (6,915,000 km²).

THE AMAZON RIVER TRAVELS THROUGH SIX DIFFERENT COUNTRIES:

- Brazil
- Peru
- Bolivia
- Venezuela
- Ecuador
- Colombia

LIFE IN THE RIVER

1,500 species of fish have been found in the Amazon River, but many more remain unidentified. The Nile River has more than **100 species of fish**.

 = 100 species

NILE

= 1,500 species

AMAZON

The river is not just home to fish. One of the largest crocodiles, the black caiman, lives there. They can grow up to **19.6 ft. (6 m)**—that's over three times longer than a human!

AMAZON RIVER DOLPHIN

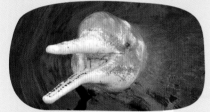

WHAT IT EATS:

AMAZON MANATEE

WHAT IT EATS:

RED-BELLIED PIRANHA

WHAT IT EATS:

FOOD CHAIN

108 feet (33 m)   8.2 feet (2.5 m)
9.1 feet (2.8 m)

LENGTH

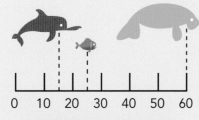

0   10   20   30   40   50   60

LIFESPAN IN YEARS

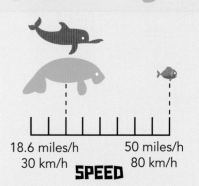

18.6 miles/h
30 km/h

50 miles/h
80 km/h

SPEED

3,000 EDIBLE FRUITS

There are at least 3,000 edible fruits in the tropical rain forests.

= 100 fruit

Tribes within the rain forest use over **2,000** fruits.

In the rest of the world, only **200** of these fruits are used.

= 3,000 fruit

We eat many fruits, vegetables, and nuts that originally came from tropical rain forests.

 ORANGES   **AVOCADOS** **PINEAPPLES**   **PEPPERS**   **FIGS**   **NUTS**

100,000,000,000 bananas are eaten each year.

THE WORLD'S LARGEST PHARMACY

Around **25% of medicines** have been developed from tropical rain forest plants.

25%

Some scientists believe that only **4%** of rain forest plants have been tested for use within medicine.

In the remaining **96%** there may be plants that could hold the cure for many diseases.

THE KAPOK TREE

The kapok tree is one of the tallest trees in tropical rain forests. It is also one of the most useful plants. Every part of it is able to be used for different purposes.

THE SEED COVERING is used in pillows and mattresses.
SEED OIL from seeds is used as soap.

THE FLOWERS are edible raw and taste like marshmallows.

THE STAMENS are often added to curries and soups for coloring.

RESIN FROM THE LEAVES, SEEDS, AND BARK is used to treat dysentery, asthma, fever, and kidney disease.

MANY TRIBES USE THE TRUNK of the kapok tree to make canoes.

THE ROOTS can be eaten once roasted.

SEEDS

Most of the plants in the rain forest grow from seeds. When a plant produces seeds, they often need to be scattered away from the mother plant to find space and food to grow.

There are many different ways that seeds travel around the rain forests.

Animals transport seeds on their fur and in their poo.

Some seeds fall into the river, floating and traveling to new locations.

The wind blows seeds off trees.

Some seeds explode out of plant pods and scatter over the ground.

The majority of the world's monkey species can be found in tropical rain forests. There are two main categories of monkey: New World monkeys and Old World monkeys. The main differences between the two groups are location and a prehensile tail.

WHAT IS A PREHENSILE TAIL?

A prehensile tail is a tail that is able to hold onto objects. New World monkeys have prehensile tails and are able to cling onto trees with them, whereas this ability is lacking in Old World monkeys—some Old World monkeys don't even have a tail.

NEW WORLD MONKEYS

They live in the rain forests of Central and South America.

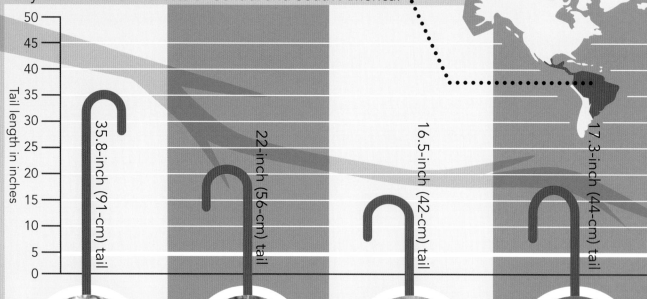

Tail length in inches: 50 45 40 35 30 25 20 15 10 5 0

35.8-inch (91-cm) tail

22-inch (56-cm) tail

16.5-inch (42-cm) tail

17.3-inch (44-cm) tail

THE HOWLER MONKEY is so-called because it can make a howling noise that can be heard up to **3 miles** (4.8 km) away.

THE CAPUCHIN MONKEY lives almost all of its life up in the trees, only coming to the ground to find water. It can jump as far as **3 yards** (2.75 m) from tree to tree.

SQUIRREL MONKEYS are incredibly sociable animals that hang around in packs of **40** to **50**, although there has been a recorded sighting of a group numbering around **500**!

TAMARIN MONKEYS have distinctive facial hair, ranging from a white handlebar moustache to a full mane of golden hair.

OLD WORLD MONKEYS

They are found in Africa and Asia, but not all live in tropical rain forests; some live in grassland and some in mountainous areas that receive heavy snow.

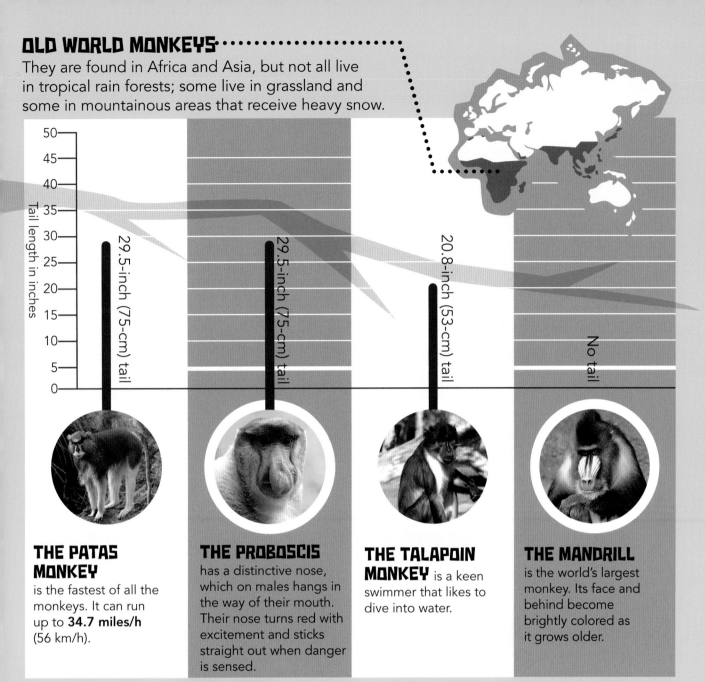

Tail length in inches

50
45
40
35
30
25
20
15
10
5
0

29.5-inch (75-cm) tail

29.5-inch (75-cm) tail

20.8-inch (53-cm) tail

No tail

THE PATAS MONKEY
is the fastest of all the monkeys. It can run up to **34.7 miles/h** (56 km/h).

THE PROBOSCIS
has a distinctive nose, which on males hangs in the way of their mouth. Their nose turns red with excitement and sticks straight out when danger is sensed.

THE TALAPOIN MONKEY
is a keen swimmer that likes to dive into water.

THE MANDRILL
is the world's largest monkey. Its face and behind become brightly colored as it grows older.

MONKEYS AND GREAT APES

They may swing from the trees, but gorillas and lemurs are not monkeys.

LEMURS

LARISES

TARSIERS

NEW WORLD MONKEYS

PROSIMIANS

OLD WORLD MONKEYS

GIBBONS

ORANGUTANS

GORILLAS

GREAT APES

CHIMPANZEES

137 PLANT, ANIMAL, AND INSECT SPECIES DIE EACH DAY

Some experts estimate that 137 plant, animal, and insect species are becoming extinct every day.

THAT'S OVER FIVE LIVING THINGS WIPED OUT EVERY HOUR.

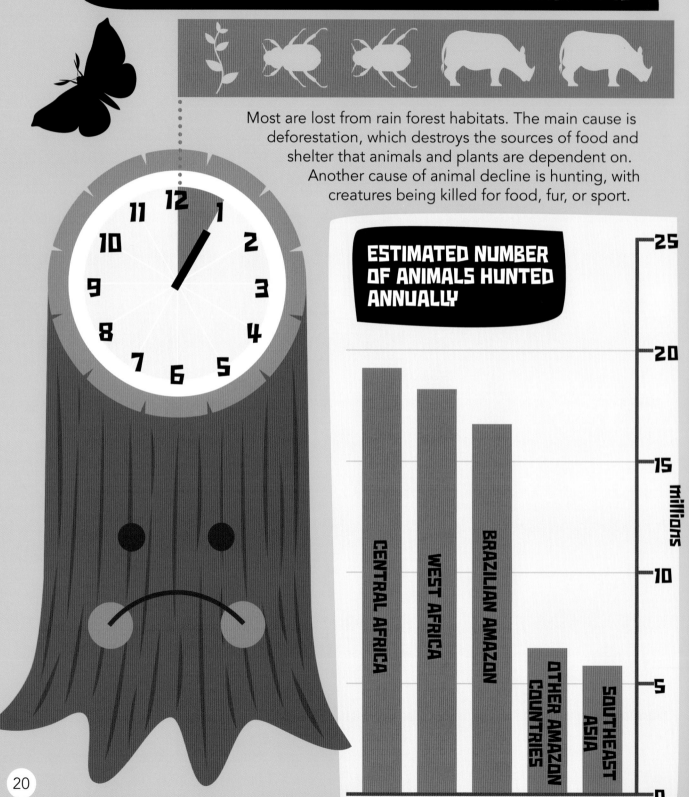

Most are lost from rain forest habitats. The main cause is deforestation, which destroys the sources of food and shelter that animals and plants are dependent on. Another cause of animal decline is hunting, with creatures being killed for food, fur, or sport.

ESTIMATED NUMBER OF ANIMALS HUNTED ANNUALLY

millions

25

20

15

10

5

0

CENTRAL AFRICA

WEST AFRICA

BRAZILIAN AMAZON

OTHER AMAZON COUNTRIES

SOUTHEAST ASIA

CRITICALLY ENDANGERED ANIMALS

If a life-form is critically endangered, it means that there are not many left and it is near extinction.

MOUNTAIN GORILLA

THREATS:
- Deforestation: use of land for agriculture and trees for firewood
- Hunting for meat, trophies
- Human diseases
- Illegal animal trade

Weight: **485 pounds** (220 kg)
Height: **5.9 feet** (1.8 m)

FEWER THAN 820 MOUNTAIN GORILLAS REMAIN.

JAVAN RHINO

FEWER THAN 50 JAVAN RHINOS REMAIN.

Weight: **5,070 pounds**
Length: **13.1 feet** (4 m)
Height: **5.5 feet** (1.7 m)

In October 2011, the last existing Javan rhino in Vietnam was found shot dead. The horn had been removed from the head. Many hunters view a rhino horn as a trophy. It is also used in some traditional Asian medicines. Rhino horn is said to be worth **$60,000 per 2.2 pounds** (1kg). That's more than twice the price of gold. By 2031 all rhino species worldwide are expected to be extinct.

RIP

EXTINCT

DIGERUS GIBBERULUS
Died: 1996
A land snail that lived in the Brazilian rain forests.

SANTALUM FERNANDEZIUM
Died: 1908
A flowering tree that grew in the forests of India, Australia, South America, and Indonesia.

GLAUCOUS MACAW
Died: 1994
A blue parrot from the South American rain forest.

KONA GIANT LOOPER MOTH
Died: 1900s
A large moth from the forests of Hawaii.

88% HUMIDITY

Humidity refers to the amount of water vapor that is in the air. You can't see water vapor, but you can feel it. The more water vapor in the air, the more the air feels damp and wet.

100% HUMIDITY
Wet, thick, fog-like atmosphere

88% HUMIDITY
Rain forest level of humidity

50% HUMIDITY
Recommended humidity level for the home

0% HUMIDITY
Completely dry

In the tropical rain forests, the humidity level is high. This means that even when it isn't raining, the atmosphere in the rain forest is always wet.

EARLY MORNING:
The skies are clear, and the air is cool. As the Sun rises, so too does the temperature.

LATE MORNING:
It is very hot and water evaporates from the forest. As the hot air rises, it cools, and the water vapor condenses to form clouds.

MIDAFTERNOON:
Clouds are now full of moisture. A thunderstorm starts and there is a heavy downpour of rain.

EARLY EVENING:
The storm is over and the air is cooler. The daily pattern is complete and ready to start again in the morning.

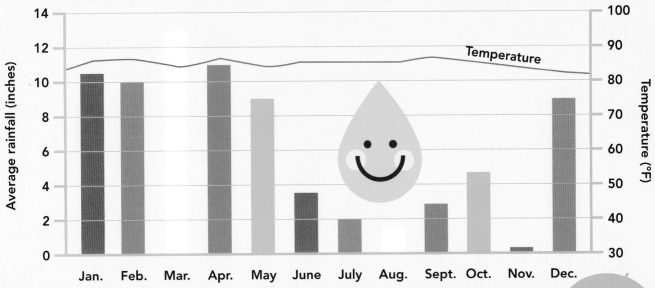

The annual amount of rainfall in the Amazon rain forest is around **82.8 inches** (2,104 mm).

WATER CYCLE

The water cycle in the tropical rain forest means that water is either falling as rain or rising as water vapor. The water vapor rises through evaporation and transpiration.

Evaporation: this happens when the heat from the Sun turns water into vapor.

Transpiration: is when plants release water from their leaves to help keep them cool.

SUN

CLOUD

CLOUD

HEAT FROM THE SUN

RAIN

10% TRANSPIRATION

Total water rising as vapor

90% EVAPORATION

23

28% OF THE WORLD'S OXYGEN

Tropical rain forests are often called "the lungs of the world." They absorb carbon dioxide and recycle it into oxygen. However, micro-organisms on the floor of the oceans release a lot more oxygen into the world for us to breathe.

70% OXYGEN PRODUCED BY OCEAN FLOOR ORGANISMS

28% TROPICAL RAIN FORESTS

2% OTHER

PHOTOSYNTHESIS

Oxygen comes from rain forest plants in a process called **photosynthesis**.

Plants use energy from the Sun to convert water and carbon dioxide from the air into sugar and oxygen.

The green color that you see in plants is created by a pigment called chlorophyll. Chlorophyll is able to capture energy from the Sun's light and use it to produce sugar. Plants use and store sugar as energy to help them grow. Animals eat the plants for their energy, which helps them to grow.

PHOTOSYNTHESIS COMES FROM THE GREEK:

PHOTO = LIGHT

SYNTHESIS =

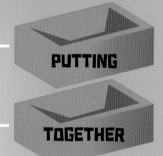

PUTTING

TOGETHER

LIGHT ENERGY FROM THE SUN

CARBON DIOXIDE FROM THE AIR

OXYGEN

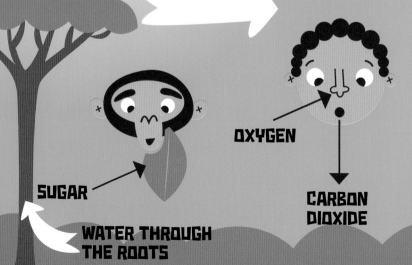

SUGAR

OXYGEN

CARBON DIOXIDE

WATER THROUGH THE ROOTS

OXYGEN

Oxygen is essential for living creatures. It is represented in science as the symbol O_2.

Oxygen is also present in water, which is represented as H_2O. A single, fully grown tree can release enough oxygen to support two human beings.

CARBON DIOXIDE

Humans and animals breathe out carbon dioxide. It is represented in science as the symbol CO_2. Too much carbon dioxide in the atmosphere is bad for the environment. Some scientists estimate that roughly **30%** of carbon dioxide released in the air comes from burning the rain forests.

THE GREENHOUSE EFFECT

The greenhouse effect is caused by greenhouse gases trapping the Sun's heat on Earth. Greenhouse gases include water vapor and carbon dioxide, which kept at certain levels, make life possible on Earth. However, the large amounts of carbon dioxide produced by burning forests cause more heat to be trapped. As a result, the average temperature on Earth rises. This has an impact on climate change, increasing the likelihood of droughts and the melting of the polar ice caps.

15-YEAR
LIFE SPAN OF THE POISON DART FROG

Poison dart frogs are found in the rain forests of Central and South America. Poison dart frogs are so-called because some South American tribes used to use the toxic secretions from the frogs to poison the tips of blow darts.

In over **175 species**, only **three** were used for this purpose.

THEY ARE THE MOST TOXIC VERTEBRATE ON EARTH.

The golden poison dart frog from Colombia can produce enough toxins to kill **10 people** or **20,000 mice**. The equivalent of just two grains of table salt (less than **1 mg**) flowing in a person's bloodstream can cause death in minutes.

x 20,000

It's believed that the poison is created by their particular diet of plants and insects. Those bred in captivity have a different diet, so are less poisonous.

The bright colors act as a warning to potential predators that they are dangerous to eat.

Poison dart frogs feed mostly on spiders, ants, and termites, which they capture with their long, sticky tongues.

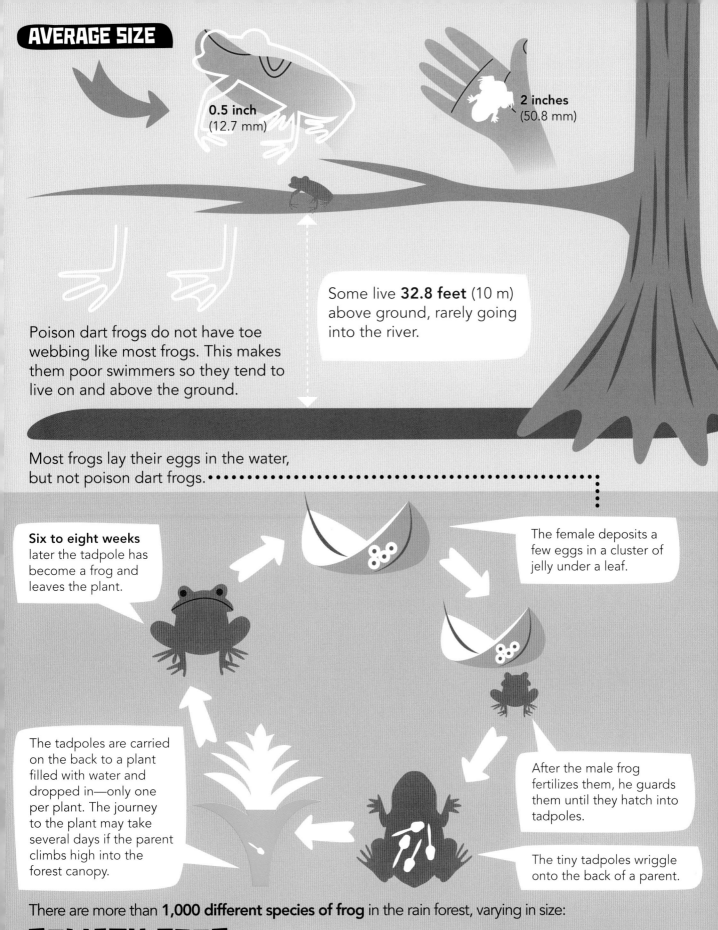

AVERAGE SIZE

0.5 inch
(12.7 mm)

2 inches
(50.8 mm)

Poison dart frogs do not have toe webbing like most frogs. This makes them poor swimmers so they tend to live on and above the ground.

Some live **32.8 feet** (10 m) above ground, rarely going into the river.

Most frogs lay their eggs in the water, but not poison dart frogs.

Six to eight weeks later the tadpole has become a frog and leaves the plant.

The female deposits a few eggs in a cluster of jelly under a leaf.

The tadpoles are carried on the back to a plant filled with water and dropped in—only one per plant. The journey to the plant may take several days if the parent climbs high into the forest canopy.

After the male frog fertilizes them, he guards them until they hatch into tadpoles.

The tiny tadpoles wriggle onto the back of a parent.

There are more than **1,000 different species of frog** in the rain forest, varying in size:

GOLIATH FROG
13 inches (33 cm)

LEMUR LEAF FROG
1.18 inches (3 cm)

FOUR LAYERS OF THE RAIN FOREST

The rain forest consists of four layers. Each layer has animal and plant life that are adapted to the conditions found there.

THE EMERGENT LAYER

contains a small number of trees that can grow up to **197 feet** (60 m). Trees that grow into this layer have long, straight trunks with branches that spread out wide at the top. Eagles, toucans, macaws, and other birds can be seen flying in the treetops.

THE CANOPY

is the densest layer of the rain forest. Trees here can grow up to **148 feet** (45 m).

THE ACAI BERRY grows on the acai palm tree and can be found in clumps hanging in the understory layer. The berry only stays ripe for approximately **24 hours**. If not eaten it will fall onto the forest floor.

DECOMPOSERS such as termites, earthworms, and fungi inhabit the forest floor. Dead leaves fall here and are digested by the decomposers, releasing the nutrients they contain back into the soil. What may take one year to decompose in an average climate takes six weeks here.

THE HARPY EAGLE lives in the emergent layer. It can live up to **35 years of age**. The eagle may swoop down into the canopy layer for food and is partial to a nice bit of sloth.

The amount of **SUNLIGHT** each rain forest layer receives affects how much life lives there and how high and dense the plants are:

100% SUNLIGHT

EMERGENT: 150–200 feet (45–60 m)

THE SLOTH lives in the canopy. It can live up to **30 years of age**. When it's feeling energetic, it reaches down into the understory to grab some acai berries to eat slowly.

25% of all insect species can be found here

70%–90% OF RAIN FOREST LIFE LIVES IN THE CANOPY

95% SUNLIGHT

CANOPY: 65–150 feet (20–45 m)

THE UNDERSTORY is the bottom third of the total height of the rain forest. Plants in the understory can grow up to **66 feet** (20 m).

FOREST FLOOR
This is where leaves and branches that fall from the trees are broken down by insects and fungi. Some small shrubs may grow up to **26 feet** (8 m).

5% SUNLIGHT

UNDERSTORY: 25–65 feet (8–20 m)

FOREST FLOOR: 0–26 feet (8 m)

0.5% SUNLIGHT

FURTHER INFORMATION

BOOKS

Eco Alert! Rainforests by Rebecca Hunter (Franklin Watts, 2012)
Explore! Rainforests by Jen Green (Wayland, 2012)
River Adventures: Amazon by Paul Manning (Franklin Watts, 2012)
Travelling Wild: Journey Along the Amazon by Alex Woolf (Wayland, 2013)

WEBSITES

Website containing information on the environmental issues
surrounding tropical rain forests:
kids.mongabay.com/
Photos from National Geographic with links to profiles on
rain forest animals:
kids.nationalgeographic.co.uk/kids/photos/tropical-rainforests/
Games, activities, and stories on the rain forest:
www.rainforest-alliance.org.uk/kids

Note to parents and teachers:
Every effort has been made by the publisher to ensure that these websites contain no
inappropriate or offensive material. However, because of the nature of the Internet, it is
impossible to guarantee that the content of these sites will not be altered. We strongly
advise that Internet access is supervised by a responsible adult.

LARGE NUMBERS

1,000,000,000,000,000,000,000,000,000,000,000 = ONE DECILLION
1,000,000,000,000,000,000,000,000,000,000 = ONE NONILLION
1,000,000,000,000,000,000,000,000,000 = ONE OCTILLION
1,000,000,000,000,000,000,000,000 = ONE SEPTILLION
1,000,000,000,000,000,000,000 = ONE SEXTILLION
1,000,000,000,000,000,000 = ONE QUINTILLION
1,000,000,000,000,000 = ONE QUADRILLION
1,000,000,000,000 = ONE TRILLION
1,000,000,000 = ONE BILLION
1,000,000 = ONE MILLION
1,000 = ONE THOUSAND
100 = ONE HUNDRED
10 = TEN
1 = ONE

GLOSSARY

amphibian	cold-blooded vertebrate that lives both on land and in water
chlorophyll	a green pigment found in plants that is able to trap light from the Sun and convert it into sugar
climate	average weather conditions in a particular area
decomposers	organisms such as fungus and earthworms that break down and feed off dead plants and animals
deforestation	the cutting down and removal of trees in a forested area
dysentery	a disease characterized by diarrhea that contains mucus and blood
endangered	at risk of extinction
equator	an imaginary line drawn around Earth separating the Northern and Southern Hemispheres
estimate	an approximate calculation
evaporation	a process whereby a liquid becomes vapor
evolutionary tree	the idea that all life has grown into new life-forms in the same way that a tree grows branches
extinct	having no living members; species that has died out
fertilizer	substance added to soil to increase plant growth
habitat	the environment or home of a creature or plant
humidity	amount of water vapor in the air
Industrial Revolution	a period when society began using machines and factories for producing goods, approximately between 1750–1850
infertile	not productive or able to produce life or grow plants
livestock	farm animals that are bought, sold, and reared for commercial reasons
logging	the work of cutting down trees
malaria	an infectious disease that causes fevers carried by mosquitoes
mammal	warm-blooded vertebrate
mercury	a silvery-white liquid metal
natural resources	material that is natural to Earth and able to be used
nutrients	a substance that is beneficial to growth and well-being
photosynthesis	the process by which plants create their own food and produce oxygen
plantation	an area where a specific crop is grown on a large scale
prehensile	capable of grasping around an object
reptile	a cold-blooded, air-breathing vertebrate
reserve	a piece of land that has been set aside for a specific purpose
species	category of living things that contains shared characteristics
stamen	the fertilizing organ of a plant
temperate	having a mild climate
toxic	a poisonous substance
transpiration	when water vapor is released from a plant
tributary	a river or stream that flows into a larger river
tropical	having a hot climate
vertebrate	a creature that has a spinal column
water vapor	water that at a certain temperature becomes invisible but is still felt as a wet element in the air

INDEX

Akuntsu, the 11
Amazon (river) 14–15
amphibians 5, 26–27
Antarctica 8
ants 6, 26
apes, great 19

beetles 6, 7
    longhorn 7
    titan 7
berries, acai 28, 29
birds 5, 21, 28
Brazil 10, 11, 12, 14, 20, 21
bugs 6
butterflies 5, 6

canopy 7, 27, 28, 29
carbon dioxide 24, 25
climate 8, 9, 28
crocodiles, black caiman 15

decomposers 28
deforestation 11, 12–13, 20, 21
Digerus gibberulus 21
diseases 11, 16, 17, 21
dolphins, Amazon river 15

eagles, harpy 29
effect, greenhouse 25
emergent layer 28, 29
endangered, critically 21
equator 4
estimates 4, 5
evaporation 22, 23
extinctions 11, 20–21

farming 12, 21
fish 15
forest (floor) 7, 12, 28, 29
frogs, poison dart 26–27
fruit 16–17

gold miners 11
gorillas 19
    mountain 21
greenhouse effect 25

humidity 4, 22–23
hunting 20, 21

Industrial Revolution 13
insects 5, 6–7, 20, 21, 26, 29

languages, tribal 10

lemurs 19
livestock 12
logging 12

macaws, glaucous 21
mammals 5, 18–19, 29
manatees, Amazon 15
medicines 11, 16–17, 21
micro-organisms 24
monkeys 18–19
    capuchin 18
    howler 18
    mandrill 19
    patas 19
    proboscis 19
    squirrel 18
    talapoin 19
    tamarin 18
moths 6
    Kona giant looper 21

oxygen 24, 25

peoples, tribal 10–11 see also tribes
photosynthesis 24
piranhas, red-bellied 15
plants, flowering 5, 21, 26
plants, medicinal 11, 16, 17

rain forests, temperate 4, 6–9
rain forests, tropical 4, 6–29
    layers of 28–29
reptiles 5, 15
rhinos, Javan 21
rivers 14–15

Santalum fernandezium 21
sloths 29

transpiration 23
trees 5, 6, 7, 8, 11, 12, 17, 18, 19, 21, 24, 25, 28–29
    kapok 17
tribes 10–11, 12, 16, 17, 26
tropics 4

understory 28, 29

Venezuela 10, 14

wood, fuel 12, 21

Yanomami, the 10, 11

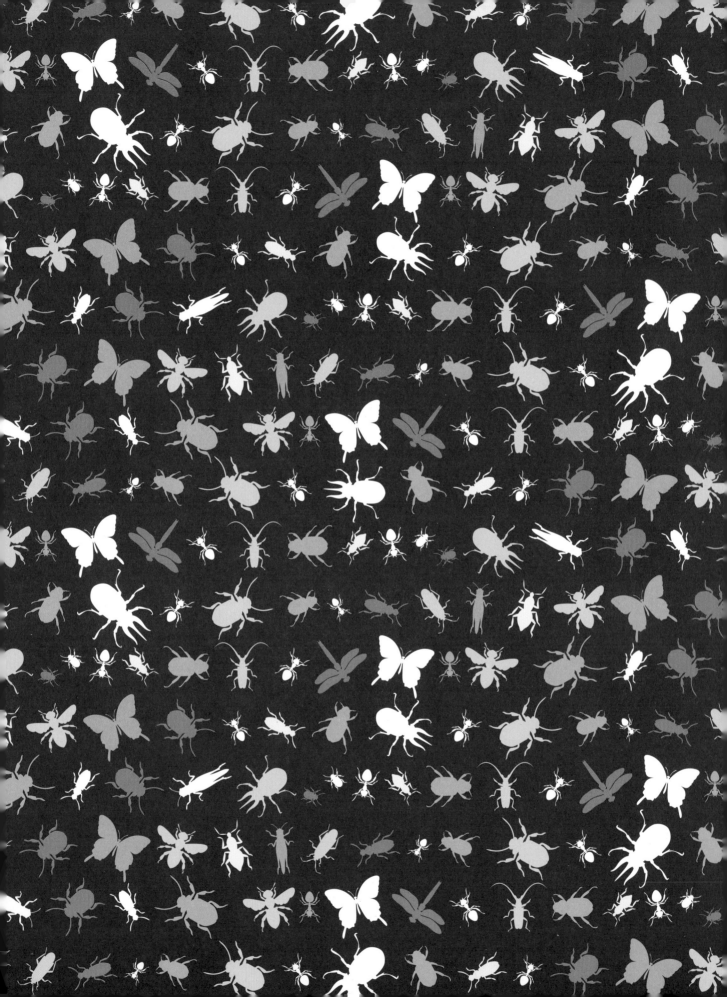